Thank You, Mom

*You can personalize this
book for your Mom!*

Find a special photograph!
Lightly glue your photo over the flowers and within the border on this page.
Make sure that your photo shows through the window of the book's front cover.

Thank You,
Mom

So here shall be
One sonnet more, a love sonnet, from me
To her whose heart is my heart's quiet home,
To my first Love, my Mother, on whose knee
I learnt love-lore that is not troublesome.

CHRISTINA ROSSETTI

Thank You, Mom

A Keepsake in Celebration of Motherhood

SPIRIT PRESS

Thank You, Mom
ISBN 1-40372-032-0

Published in 2006 by Spirit Press, an imprint of Dalmatian Press, LLC.
Copyright © 2006 Dalmatian Press, LLC. Franklin, Tennessee 37067.

Editor: Lila Empson
Writer: Jonathan Rogers
Cover and text design: Diane Whisner

06 07 08 09 LPU 10 9 8 7 6 5 4 3 2 1

14949

*My mother shared fully my
ambition and sympathized
with me and aided me in
every way she could. If I have
done anything in life worth
attention, I feel sure that
I inherited the disposition
from my mother.*

BOOKER T. WASHINGTON

Strength and dignity are her clothing,
And she smiles at the future.
She opens her mouth in wisdom,
And the teaching of kindness is on her tongue.
She looks well to the ways of her household,
And does not eat the bread of idleness.
Her children rise up and bless her.

PROVERBS 31:25–28 NASB

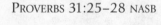

Introduction

*H*ow do I say thank you, Mom? How do I thank the person who brought me into the world, who taught me how to tie my shoes, who sent me off to school in the morning and welcomed me home again in the afternoon? How do I thank you for teaching me right from wrong and making sure I knew I was special? How do I thank you for making sure I knew that God loves me? Even now, Mom, you're still my biggest cheerleader. I can always go to you for a word of encouragement.

There's no part of my life you haven't touched. There's never a day when I don't remember something you told me, something you gave me, something you did for me. I thank God for giving me such a mother. I love you, Mom.

Honor your father and your mother, so that your days may be long in the land that the Lord your God is giving you.

EXODUS 20:12 NRSV

Heaven and earth are grand; father and mother are venerable.

Let France have good mothers,
and she will have good sons.

NAPOLEON BONAPARTE

The hand that rocks the cradle rules the world.

WILLIAM ROSS WALLACE

Mighty is the force of motherhood! It transforms all things by its vital heart.

GEORGE ELIOT

Love is patient and kind. Love is not jealous or boastful or proud or rude. Love does not demand its own way. Love is not irritable, and it keeps no record of when it has been wronged. It is never glad about injustice but rejoices whenever the truth wins out. Love never gives up, never loses faith, is always hopeful, and endures through every circumstance.

1 CORINTHIANS 13:4–7 NLT

The family is the school of duties . . .
founded on love.

FELIX ADLER

Mothers have as powerful
an influence over the welfare
of future generations, as all
other causes combined.

JOHN ABBOTT

One Mom
Remembers...

Know what I remember most about second grade? Chicken pox. Actually, I don't really remember the chicken pox. I remember being home from school. Nobody was there but you and me. I was bundled up in bed, and you were sitting in the big chair you dragged into my room. And you read to me. *Charlotte's Web*, I think it was. But the book didn't matter; it could have been the telephone book for all I cared. What mattered was that I had you all to myself. Everybody else was at school or work. And there in my bedroom, amid the stuffed animals and scattered toys, your voice lulled me to sleep and time stood still for a short while.

Those who fear the LORD are secure; he will be a place of refuge for their children.

PROVERBS 14:26 NLT

Mother's arms are made of tenderness, and sweet sleep blesses the child who lies therein.

VICTOR HUGO

Timely blossom, infant fair,
Fondling of a happy pair,
Every morn, and every night
Their solicitous delight,
Sleeping, waking, still at ease,
Pleasing, without skill to please.

AMBROSE PHILIPS

*What can be more clear and sound in explanation,
than the love of a parent to his child?*

WILLIAM GODWIN

*A mother's love! O holy boundless thing!
Fountain whose waters never cease to spring.*

LADY MARGUERITE BLESSINGTON

Make your father happy!
Make your mother proud!

PROVERBS 23:25 THE MESSAGE

*Who takes the child by
the hand takes the
mother by the heart.*

DANISH PROVERB

I remember the sincere faith you have,
the kind of faith that your grandmother
Lois and your mother Eunice also had.
I am sure that you have it also.

2 Timothy 1:5 gnt

I was placed in your care from birth. From
my mother's womb you have been my God.

Psalm 22:10 god's word

What a mother sings to the cradle goes all the way down to the coffin.

Henry Ward Beecher

*Mother is the name for God in the
lips and hearts of little children.*

WILLIAM MAKEPEACE THACKERAY

Did You Know?

Julia Ward Howe is credited as being the first person to propose a Mother's Day in America, though it wasn't exactly the Mother's Day we all know and love. In 1872 she called for a day when mothers would join together for huge anti-war demonstrations. Her other claim to fame? She wrote "The Battle Hymn of the Republic."

Mother's Day as we know it came about thanks to the efforts of Anna M. Jarvis. The first Mother's Day church service was held, at her request, on Sunday, May 10, 1908, in Grafton, West Virginia. Six years later, in 1914, Congress officially declared the second Sunday in May to be a day to honor mothers.

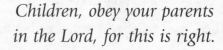

Children, obey your parents in the Lord, for this is right.

Ephesians 6:1 NASB

The ship that will not obey the helm must obey the rocks.

ENGLISH PROVERB

Before I got married, I had six theories about raising children. Now I have six children and no theories.

JOHN WILMOT

Children are unaccountable little creatures.

KATHERINE MANSFIELD

There never was a child so lovely, but his mother was glad to get him asleep.

Ralph Waldo Emerson

*Perhaps the greatest social service
that can be rendered by anybody to
the country and to mankind is to
bring up a family.*

GEORGE BERNARD SHAW

All that I am, my mother made me.

JOHN QUINCY ADAMS

*All that I am or hope to be I owe
to my angel mother.*

ABRAHAM LINCOLN

'Tis the gift to be simple; 'tis the gift to be free,
'Tis the gift to come down where we ought to be.
And when we find ourselves in the place just right,
'Twill be in the valley of love and delight.

SHAKER SONG

Survival Tip

Make a Not-to-Do List:

As a mother, you probably have a to-do list a mile long. Have you thought about making a not-to-do list too? Life gets complicated; it's important to simplify where you can, to leave more time for things that really are important. What are the things that waste your time every day? Add them to your not-to-do list. You might declare that you're not going to touch any piece of mail (other than personal letters) more than once. You might decide not to listen to the radio when you're alone in the car, so you can use that time for thinking or praying. You might decide not to check your e-mail more than twice a day. You know what wastes your time. Simplify.

The godly walk with integrity;
blessed are their children
after them.

PROVERBS 20:7 NLT

*One generation plants
the trees; another gets
the shade.*

CHINESE PROVERB

33

Never fear spoiling children by making them too happy. Happiness is the atmosphere in which all good affections grow.

ANN ELIZA BRAY

A child is fed with milk and praise.

MARY ANN LAMB

*Too much indulgence
has ruined thousands
of children; too much
love not one.*

FANNY FERN

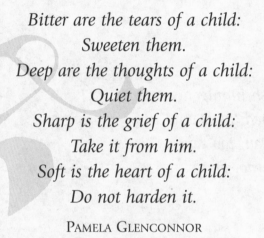

Bitter are the tears of a child:
Sweeten them.
Deep are the thoughts of a child:
Quiet them.
Sharp is the grief of a child:
Take it from him.
Soft is the heart of a child:
Do not harden it.

PAMELA GLENCONNOR

This Changes Everything

The nurse put that bundled newborn in my arms, and I thought, *Well now, this changes everything.* No single event, no one day had ever changed me so completely. The day I graduated, I didn't suddenly feel smarter. The day I got married, I didn't love my husband more than I did the day before. But the day I became a mother, the moment I looked into that pinched little face, I knew I was a different person. A mother. The name didn't quite seem to fit, and yet that surge of mother love told me that there was no other word for it.

*Hear, my child, your father's
instruction, and do not reject
your mother's teaching.*

PROVERBS 1:8 NRSV

Education commences at the mother's knee, and every word spoken within hearsay of little children tends toward the formation of character.

HOSEA BALLOU

You can learn many things from children.
How much patience you have, for instance.

FRANKLIN P. JONES

My mother had a great deal of trouble with
me, but I think she enjoyed it.

MARK TWAIN

Don't be discouraged if your children reject your advice. Years later they will offer it to their own offspring.

SOURCE UNKNOWN

You still the hunger of those you cherish;
their sons have plenty,
and they store up wealth for
their children.

PSALM 17:14 NIV

*A rich child often sits in a
poor mother's lap.*

DANISH PROVERB

*You may not be able to leave your
children a great inheritance, but
day by day, you may be weaving
coats for them which they will
wear for all eternity.*

THEODORE L. CUYLER

One Mom Remembers...

You probably don't even remember this, Mom, but I'll never forget it. I was five or six. Early one morning I noticed a light on downstairs. I followed it to the kitchen, and there you were, head bowed over an open Bible.

"What are you doing, Mommy?" I asked.

"I'm praying," you answered.

"What are you praying about?"

"Lots of things. Mostly you and your brother—for your safety, for your holiness. I pray you'll come to know Jesus. Sometimes I even pray for the people you're going to marry. Every morning. Right here at this table."

It changed my world to think of you praying for us every morning.

Pour out your heart like water
Before the presence of the Lord;
Lift your hands to Him
For the life of your little ones.

LAMENTATIONS 2:19 NASB

I remember my mother's prayers and
they have always followed me. They
have clung to me all my life.

ABRAHAM LINCOLN

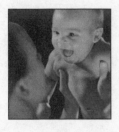

Hypocrisy in anything whatever may deceive the cleverest and most penetrating man, but the least wide-awake of children recognizes it, and is revolted by it, however ingeniously it may be disguised.

LEO TOLSTOY

You mustn't say anything that won't be perfectly true when he's grown up, you see. It's learning two sets of things that makes a child distrust you.

JOSEPHINE DODGE BACON

Children are unpredictable. You never know what inconsistency they're going to catch you in next.

FRANKLIN P. JONES

*Your mother was like a vine
in a vineyard transplanted
by the water, fruitful and
full of branches by reason of
abundant water.*

EZEKIEL 19:10 NRSV

My mother was the most beautiful woman I ever saw. All I am I owe to my mother. I attribute all my success in life to the moral, intellectual, and physical education I received from her.

GEORGE WASHINGTON

They shall not labor in vain,
Nor bring forth children for trouble;
For they shall be the descendants
of the blessed of the LORD,
And their offspring with them.

ISAIAH 65:23 NKJV

I will pour out my spirit on your children
and my blessing on your descendants.

ISAIAH 44:3 GNT

Upon her soothing breast
She lulled her little child;
A winter sunset in the west,
A dreary glory smiled.

EMILY BRONTË

I have learned more about Christianity from my mother than from all the theologians of England.

JOHN WESLEY

Did You Know?

Susanna Wesley was no stranger to suffering. She lived in the shadow of poverty, illness, and hardship. She gave birth to nineteen children, but nine of them died before the age of two. Still, she remained faithful and committed herself to teaching her children the things of God. Though her huge family was squeezed into a tiny house, she valued quiet time with God, and she made sure she got it. When she sat down and pulled her apron over her head, her children knew not to disturb her: she was praying. Her faithfulness paid huge dividends. One of her sons, John, went on to found the Methodist Church. Another son, Charles, wrote over nine thousand hymns and remains one of the best-loved hymnists of all time.

*Cast all your anxieties
on him because he
cares for you.*

1 Peter 5:7 niv

A mother's life, you see, is one long succession of dramas, now soft and tender, now terrible. Not an hour but has its joys and fears.

HONORÉ DE BALZAC

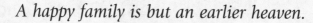

A happy family is but an earlier heaven.

JOHN BOWRING

All the wealth in the world cannot be compared with the happiness of living together happily united.

SAINT MARGUERITE D'YOUVILLE

It is in the love of one's family only that heartfelt happiness is known.

THOMAS JEFFERSON

*If you would have your son walk
honourable through the world,
you must not attempt to clear
the stones from his path, but
teach him to walk firmly over
them—not insist upon leading
him by the hand, but let him
learn to go alone.*

ANNE BRONTË

*A mother is not a person to lean upon, but a person
to make leaning unnecessary.*

DOROTHY CANFIELD

*Where parents do too much for their children, the
children will not do much for themselves.*

ELBERT HUBBARD

The best memory is not as good as pale ink.

<small>CHINESE PROVERB</small>

Survival Tip

Keep an "Out of the Mouths of Babes" Book:

When your children or grandchildren say something brilliant or hilarious, you don't think you could ever forget it. But the fact is, most people do forget most of the clever things their kids say. Keep a notebook handy to write down your kids' witticisms. It will be a source of smiles and happy memories for many years to come.

*I have calmed and quieted
my soul, like a weaned
child with its mother; my
soul is like the weaned
child that is with me.*

PSALM 131:2 NRSV

Blest the babe
Nursed in his mother's
arms, the babe who sleeps
Upon his mother's breast.

WILLIAM WORDSWORTH

When God thought of mother, he must have
laughed with satisfaction, and framed it
quickly—so rich, so deep, so divine, so full of
soul, power, and beauty, was the conception.

HENRY WARD BEECHER

A mother is a mother still,
The holiest thing alive.

SAMUEL TAYLOR COLERIDGE

*Love may be the fairest gem
which Society has filched
from Nature; but what is
motherhood save Nature in
her most gladsome mood? A
smile has dried my tears.*

HONORÉ DE BALZAC

There never was a woman like her. She was gentle as a dove and brave as a lioness. . . . The memory of my mother and her teachings were, after all, the only capital I had to start life with, and on that capital I have made my way.

ANDREW JACKSON

My Mother, My Defender

I've heard there's nothing fiercer than a mother alligator protecting her young. I've never seen a mother alligator protect her young, but I have seen my own mother do it. One summer day, some bigger boys from the neighborhood came into our yard and started picking on my sister and me. As I remember, one of them was poking a finger into my chest when we heard the screen door slam. There on the front stoop stood Mom, hands on hips. She was five-two with her shoes on, and I don't think she weighed a hundred pounds. But when those boys saw the ferocity flashing in her eyes, they didn't waste any time; they turned tail and ran. They didn't even stop to get their bikes. Later that day, after she was sure those boys' parents would be around, Mom walked those bikes home to them. I don't know what was said, but that was the last trouble we ever had from those boys.

Unless the LORD builds the house,
its builders labor in vain.

PSALM 127:1 NIV

'Mid pleasures and palaces
  though we may roam,
    Be it ever so humble,
there's no place like home.

JOHN HOWARD PAINE

*To understand your parents' love you must
raise children yourself.*

CHINESE PROVERB

*A man never sees all that his mother
has been to him until it's too late to
let her know he sees it.*

WILLIAM DEAN HOWELLS

No man is poor who had
a godly mother.

ABRAHAM LINCOLN

God pardons like a mother, who kisses the
offense into everlasting forgiveness.

HENRY WARD BEECHER

The heart of a mother is a deep abyss at the bot-
tom of which you will always find forgiveness.

HONORÉ DE BALZAC

*You, O Lord, are a merciful
and loving God, always patient,
always kind and faithful.*

PSALM 86:15 GNT

One Mom Remembers...

The kids were driving me crazy today—just regular kid stuff, but I was nearing the end of my rope. Then I remembered how patient you always were with us. Even when Chip superglued a quarter to the parquet floor in the foyer. Even when I broke that lamp after you had told me three times to stop doing cartwheels in the living room. I don't know what you had going on inside, but on the outside, you always remained calm and placid and, most of all, loving. So I took a deep breath, counted to ten, and got it back together. Just like you would have done, Mom. Thanks.

If any of you lacks wisdom, let him ask of God, who gives to all liberally and without reproach, and it will be given to him.

JAMES 1:5 NKJV

Children need models rather than critics.

JOSEPH JOUBERT

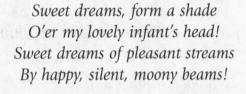

Sweet dreams, form a shade
O'er my lovely infant's head!
Sweet dreams of pleasant streams
By happy, silent, moony beams!

Sweet sleep, with soft down
Weave thy brows an infant crown!
Sweet sleep, angel mild,
Hover o'er my happy child!

Sweet smiles, in the night
Hover over my delight!
Sweet smiles, mother's smiles,
All the livelong night beguiles.

WILLIAM BLAKE

*The watchful mother tarries nigh, though
sleep has closed her infant's eyes.*

JOHN KEBLE

Mothers are the most instinctive philosophers.

HARRIET BEECHER STOWE

Even before I speak, you know
what I am going to say.

PSALM 139:4 GNT

*A mother understands
what a child does not say.*

JEWISH PROVERB

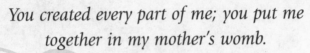

You created every part of me; you put me together in my mother's womb.

PSALM 139:13 GNT

Behold, children are a gift of the LORD,
The fruit of the womb is a reward.

PSALM 127:3 NASB

We find delight in the beauty and happiness of children that makes the heart too big for the body.

RALPH WALDO EMERSON

He that wipes the child's nose
kisseth the mother's cheek.

GEORGE HERBERT

Did You Know?

The Mother Who Changed the Course of Church History

Monica was a Christian woman living in fifth-century Northern Africa when that region was still part of the Roman Empire. In 354 A.D, she gave birth to a boy, her only child and her pride and joy. She taught the boy of Christ's love and prayed for him constantly. But as the boy grew up, he abandoned her teaching, choosing instead to pursue the worldly pleasures—as well as the pagan philosophies and religious beliefs—that were so readily available in the late Roman Empire. But through it all, Monica continued to pray for her son faithfully, convinced that God would reach him eventually. When Monica's son was thirty years old, God finally broke through. Monica's son was Saint Augustine, and the truths she taught him at her knee have echoed throughout history.

*Charm is deceptive, and
beauty is fleeting; but a
woman who fears the L*ORD
is to be praised.

PROVERBS 31:30 NIV

I wonder why you care so much about me—no, I don't wonder. I only accept is as the thing at the back of all one's life that makes everything bearable and possible.

GERTRUDE BELL
TO HER MOTHER

The babe at first feeds upon the mother's bosom, but it is always on her heart.

HENRY WARD BEECHER

Mother's love grows by giving.

CHARLES LAMB

Youth fades; love droops; the
leaves of friendship fall;
A mother's secret hope
outlives them all.

OLIVER WENDELL HOLMES

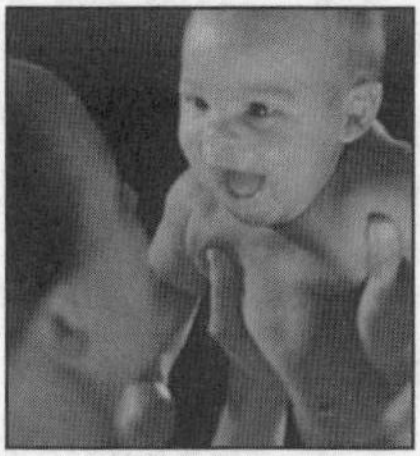

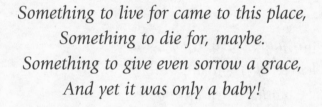

Something to live for came to this place,
Something to die for, maybe.
Something to give even sorrow a grace,
And yet it was only a baby!

HARRIET SPOFFORD

What a difference it makes to come home to a child!
MARGARET FULLER

Children are the anchors of a mother's life.
SOPHOCLES

*The goodness of the father reaches higher
than a mountain. That of the mother
goes deeper than the ocean.*

JAPANESE PROVERB

Survival Tip

*T*ake Pictures on Non-Special Occasions Too:

When do you pull out the camera? Birthday parties? School programs? Don't forget to take pictures and movies of day-to-day living too. Fifteen years from now, it will be fun to look back at the kids in their Christmas pageant costumes, but it will be even more thrilling to revisit everyday life, the way you live it right now. Record the gestures and expressions that make your kids unique. Save images of them running around in the yard, riding their bikes, playing their favorite games. And not just the kids: get pictures and movies of yourself too. It may seem less than exciting now, but it will be a treasure in years to come.

I prayed for this child, and the LORD has granted me what I asked of him.

1 SAMUEL 1:27 NIV

*Children are poor
men's riches.*

ENGLISH PROVERB

*A mother is the truest friend we have, when
trials, heavy and sudden, fall upon us;
when adversity takes the place of prosperity;
when friends who rejoice with us in our
sunshine, desert us when troubles thicken
around us, still will she cling to us, and
endeavor by her kind precepts and counsels
to dissipate the clouds of darkness, and
cause peace to return to our hearts.*

WASHINGTON IRVING

Who is it that loves me and will love me forever with an affection which no chance, no misery, no crime of mine can do away? It is you, my mother.

THOMAS CARLYLE

Only a mother's heart can be Patient enough for such as he.

ETHEL LYNN BEERS

Teach your children to choose the right path, and
when they are older, they will remain upon it.

PROVERBS 22:6 NLT

Mama Came to School

I only remember one time when Mama was visibly disappointed in me, and that was more than enough. She had come to the school one day to deliver my sister's science project and thought it would be a nice surprise if she went out to the schoolyard to see me at recess. Some boys were teasing Clifford, a boy who wasn't like the rest of us. I was right in the middle of them. I'll never forget the look of shock and sadness on Mama's face. She never said a word about it. She never had to. Let me tell you, I never again had the stomach for that kind of meanness.

Take care and watch yourselves closely, so as neither to forget the things that your eyes have seen nor to let them slip from your mind all the days of your life; make them known to your children and your children's children.

DEUTERONOMY 4:9 NRSV

*The school may do much,
but alas for the child
where the instructor is
not assisted by the
influences of home!*

HANNAH FARNHAM LEE

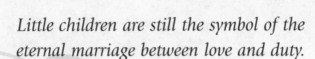

Little children are still the symbol of the eternal marriage between love and duty.

GEORGE ELIOT

A mother who is really a mother is never free.

HONORÉ DE BALZAC

No one without experience knows the anguish which children can cause and yet be loved.

ELISABETH OF BRAUNSCHWEIG

I will teach you hidden lessons from our past—
stories we have heard and know,
stories our ancestors handed down to us.
We will not hide these truths from our children
but will tell the next generation
about the glorious deeds of the LORD.
We will tell of his power and
the mighty miracles he did.

PSALM 78:2–4 NLT

O wondrous power! How little understood, entrusted to the mother's mind alone to fashion genius, for the soul for good, inspire a West, or train a Washington!

Sarah Josepha Hale

An ounce of mother is worth a pound of clergy.

Spanish Proverb

One Mom Remembers...

How many people's lives have been touched by your hospitality, Mom? Through the years you opened your home to hundreds, maybe thousands of people—half of whom you weren't even expecting. Growing up, my friends always thought our house was the place to be. I was so proud to have such a mom. I think everybody wished their moms were more like you—so welcoming, so loving, so unworried about the little messes that go along with having extra people in the house. I get so stressed out when people are coming over. How did you do it, Mom?

Don't forget to show hospitality to strangers,
for some who have done this have entertained
angels without realizing it!

HEBREWS 13:2 NLT

According to my method of thinking, and that of many others, not woman but the mother is the most precious possession of the nation, so precious that society advances its highest well-being when it protects the functions of the mother.

<small>ELLEN KEY</small>

The future destiny of the child is always the work of the mother.

NAPOLEON BONAPARTE

Men are what their mothers made them.

RALPH WALDO EMERSON

*Never forget these commands
that I am giving you today.
Teach them to your children.
Repeat them when you are at
home and when you are
away, when you are resting
and when you are working.*

DEUTERONOMY 6:6–7 GNT

The mother's heart is the child's schoolroom.

HENRY WARD BEECHER

*Make our sons in their prime like sturdy
oak trees, Our daughters as shapely and
bright as fields of wildflowers.*

PSALM 144:12 THE MESSAGE

*Your descendants will become
well-known all over.
Your children in foreign countries
Will be recognized at once
as the people I have blessed.*

ISAIAH 61:9 THE MESSAGE

We bear the world, and we make it. . . . There was never a great man who had not a great mother—it is hardly an exaggeration.

OLIVE SCHREINER

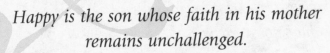

Happy is the son whose faith in his mother remains unchallenged.

Louisa May Alcott

Did You Know?

Mother's Day is the busiest day of the year for restaurants. It's also the busiest day of the year for long-distance phone calls (though not for collect calls—that's Father's Day). Mother's Day is the third-biggest greeting card holiday, behind Christmas and Valentine's Day.

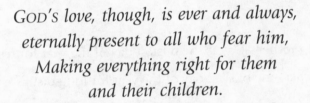

GOD's love, though, is ever and always,
eternally present to all who fear him,
Making everything right for them
and their children.

PSALM 103:17 THE MESSAGE

A mother's heart is always
with her children.

What do girls do who haven't any mothers to help them through their troubles?

LOUISA MAY ALCOTT

My daughter's my daughter all her life.

DINAH MARIA MULOCK CRAIK

*I am always button-holing
somebody and saying, "Someday
you must meet my mother."
And then I am off. And nothing
stops me till the waiters close up
the café. I do love you so much,
my mother. . . . If I didn't keep
calling you mother, anybody
reading this would think I was
writing to my sweetheart. And
he would be quite right.*

EDNA ST. VINCENT MILLAY

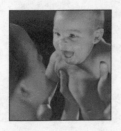

Women know
The way to rear up children (to be just),
They know a simple, merry, tender knack
Of tying sashes, fitting baby-shoes,
And stringing pretty words that make no sense,
And kissing full sense into empty words.

ELIZABETH BARRETT BROWNING

Who ran to help me when I fell,
And would some pretty story tell,
Or kiss the place to make it well?
My mother.

JANE TAYLOR

Children should be led into the right paths,
not by severity, but by persuasion.

TERENCE

There is no mother like your own mother.

BAMBARA PROVERB

Survival Tip

*E*at Together:

The leisurely meal with the whole family sitting around the dinner table is becoming more and more of a rarity. Especially as kids get well into their school years, they have busy schedules that take them in many different directions. But it's worth the effort to get everybody to the table. Studies show that eating with other people improves nutrition for people of all ages. Even more important, family meals build strong families. There's no better place to communicate as a family.

Be very careful how you live.
Don't live like foolish people
but like wise people.

EPHESIANS 5:15 GOD'S WORD

*Children are made of eyes
and ears, and nothing,
however minute, escapes
their microscopic observation.*

FANNY KEMBLE

To be happy at home is the ultimate result of all ambition.

Samuel Johnson

For unflagging interest and enjoyment, a household of children, if things go reasonably well, certainly makes all other forms of success and achievement lose their importance by comparison.

Theodore Roosevelt

*Where there is a mother in
the home, matters go well.*

AMOS BRONSON ALCOTT